Intentional

Workbook

Jessica Ullyott

Table Of Contents

Activity	Page
Sustainable Lifestyle Questionnaire	2-3
Growing Appreciation Worksheet	4-5
Food Supply Chain	6-7
Goal Setting Worksheet	8
Youth Goal Setting Worksheet	9
Cognitive Hierarchy	10-11
Zero Waste Audit	12-13
Just for Fun	14-25
Dirty Dozen & Clean Fifteen	27
How to Sort Your Waste	29
Produce Storage Guide	31
Meal Planners & Shopping Lists	33-38
Snack Recipes	41-48
Personal Care Recipes	49-58
Cleaning Recipes	59-69
About the Author/Illustrator	71

Sustainable Lifestyle Questionnaire

1. Circle words or phrases that you are familiar with:

Zero Waste

Biodiversity hotspot

Compost

Vermicompost

Bokashi

Stewardship

Refillery

Zero waste grocery

Repurpose

Wishcycling

Carbon footprint

Carbon offset

Recycle contamination

Carbon Sink

2. How informed do you personally feel you are about recycling and composting?

Very informed

Somewhat informed

Not informed

Unsure

3. How much does your family recycle?

Often

Sometimes

Rarely

Never

4. Have you researched what can be recycled in your area?

Yes

Somewhat

No

5. Does your area offer organic recycling?

Yes

No

Not Sure

6. How often do you think to reuse or repurpose an item?

Often

Sometimes

Rarely

Never

7. When an item breaks do you...
Fix it
Find a new use for it
Throw it away

8. How often do you think of buying an item that is packaged in paper or glass instead of plastic?
Often
Sometimes
Rarely
Never
Don't know

9. Which reusable items do you carry with you?
Napkin
Water Bottle
Straw
Silverware
Shopping bag
Plate
Cup

10. Which of these does your family currently do?
Walk or bike to destinations
Reuse items (jars, bottles, ect.)
Carry reusable water bottles, straws or silverware
Use refill services (shops, personal products, ect.)
Shop used (Offer Up, Nextdoor, thrift stores, ect.)
Use cloth diapers (if applicable)
Use cloth napkins instead of paper napkins
Use towels instead of paper towels
Volunteer for environmental stewardship
Donate items instead of throwing them away
Repurpose items instead of throwing them away
Recycle organic waste

Growing Appreciation Practice

In this exercise you will be using your 5 senses to grow your appreciation for the living things outside your home. I would recommend you bring something with you that you can drink that will help you relax in this moment like a cup of coffee or tea. You will also need something to draw with like a pencil or colored markers if you choose.

- Begin by finding a space outside. This can be in your yard, a park or an open space.
- Take some time to feel gratitude for this moment. You can choose to close your eyes, place your hand on your chest or on the ground.
- Take note of what you smell. Is there anything around you that you brought with you or that you can easily walk to and smell? A plant? A cup of coffee?
- Take note of how your drink tastes. Does it taste light or dark? Can you imagine the plant from which it came?
- Take note of what you see. What color are the plants this time of year? Are there any clouds in the sky?
- Take note of what you hear. Are there any birds? Do you hear any people or airplanes?
- Take note of the textures around you. What do the plants nearby feel like? What is on the ground? Is it cold, wet, soft, rough?

Use the space below to either list out some of the things you noticed or are grateful for. If you would rather, you could also compose a poem or other verse to express yourself.

____

____

____

____

____

____

____

____

____

____

____

Next, take a moment to find something nearby that you would like to spend some time with. This can be a plant, a leaf, a rock, ect. Begin by simply examining the item for 5 minutes. No drawing allowed. Try to keep your focus on the item.
After 5 minutes, you can begin to draw your subject. This is not about perfection. It is about connecting with it and the space you are in. Take as much time as you need.

Food Supply Chain

1. What do you know about your current food supply chain (where you get your food)?
Circle the choices below to complete the chain:

Origin ⟶ **Processing** ⟶ **Transportation** ⟶ **Destination**

Origin	Processing	Transportation	Destination
• Local Farm • Domestic Farm • Foreign Farm	• Factory to be processed and packaged • Packaged by farm	• Delivered by trucks or train • Delivered by aircraft or ship and then trucks or train • Transported by farmer	• Big-Box retailer • Family owned retailer • Farmers Market • Delivered to your home

2. Would you say your current food system is sustainable*? Why or why not?

____

____

____

____

____

____

____

____

____

____

Consider that there is food waste during each phase of the supply chain. Imperfect food that is not sold, food that is damaged during processing and packaging, food that is not sold in time and rots, and food that is purchased and then not eaten in time before it rots.

3. What elements of a more regional, sustainable food system do you see in your area that you could explore?

____

____

____

____

____

____

____

____

____

____

Goal Setting Worksheet

What are sustainable things you are already doing?

- ____
- ____
- ____
- ____
- ____
- ____

To build a more sustainable lifestyle, I could...

- ____
- ____
- ____
- ____
- ____

Goal #1

One thing I am going to start doing is...
- ____

I'll start doing this on _______ (date) and work on it until _______ (date).

One way I'll know I'm getting better is...
- ____

Goal #2

One thing I am going to start doing is...
- ____

I'll start doing this on _______ (date) and work on it until _______ (date).

One way I'll know I'm getting better is...
- ____

Adapted from Figure 4.12 of Chappuis, J. (2015). Seven strategies of assessment for learning. Pearson.

Youth Goal Setting Worksheet

What are sustainable things that you are already doing?

- ____
- ____
- ____
- ____
- ____

GOAL	STEPS	EVIDENCE
WHAT SUSTAINABLE HABITS COULD I WORK ON?	HOW DO I PLAN TO DO THIS?	WHAT EVIDENCE WILL SHOW I'VE ACHIEVED MY GOAL?

**Who can I review my sustainable choices and goals with?
(Friends, family, or trusted adult)**

- ____
- ____
- ____

Adapted from Figure 4.12 of Chappuis, J. (2015). Seven strategies of assessment for learning. Pearson.

Cognitive Hierarchy

Using this modified pyramid, write down some of your or your families values regarding sustainability and then determine what the norm is in your home and the behaviors you see exhibited by you and/or your family. Focus on one value at a time.

For example, here is a completed one regarding "family communication"

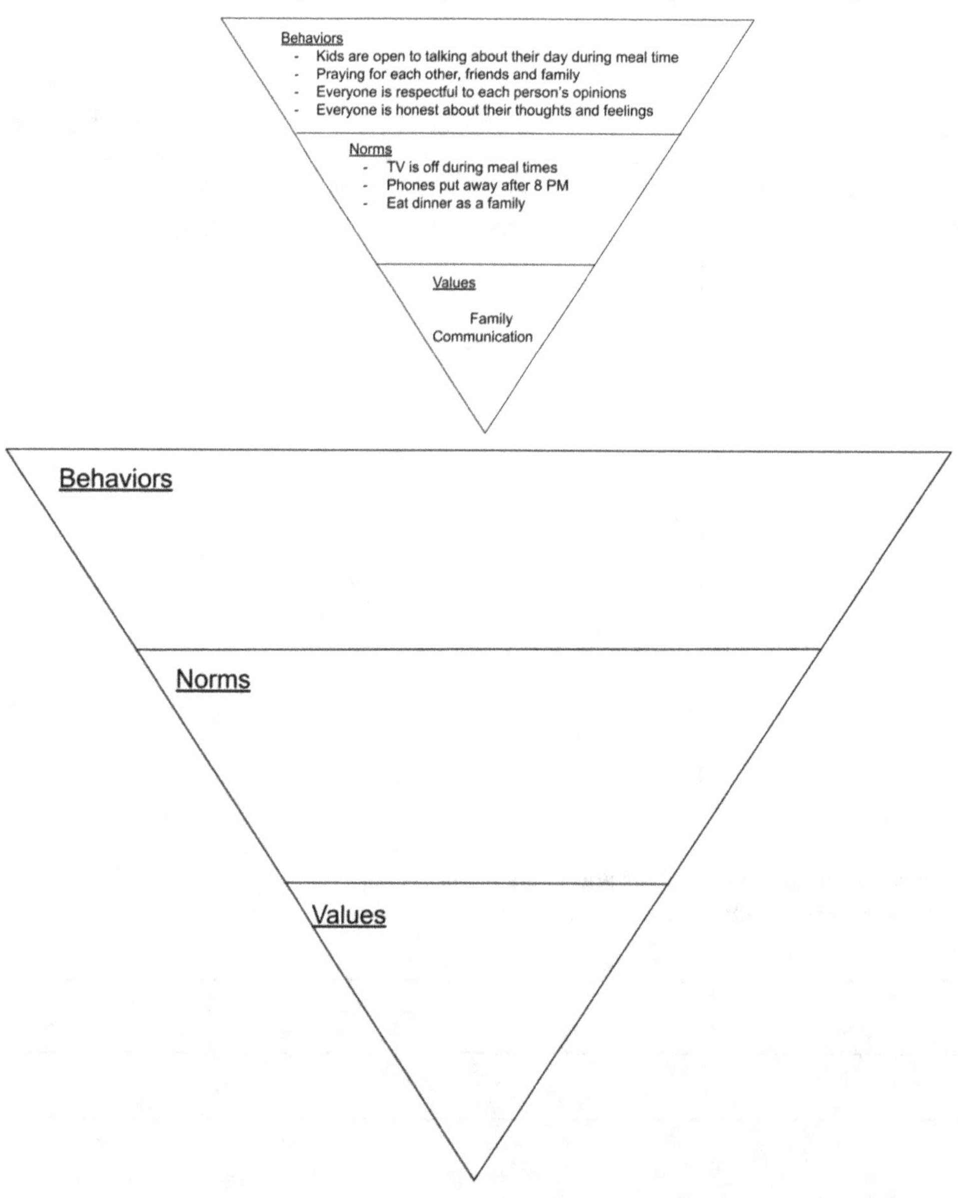

How would you like to see your or your family's behaviors change? Remember that it is not about changing the value per se, it's about finding a way to mesh these new ideas to values that you already have. Fill out the chart below to get an idea of how this would look:

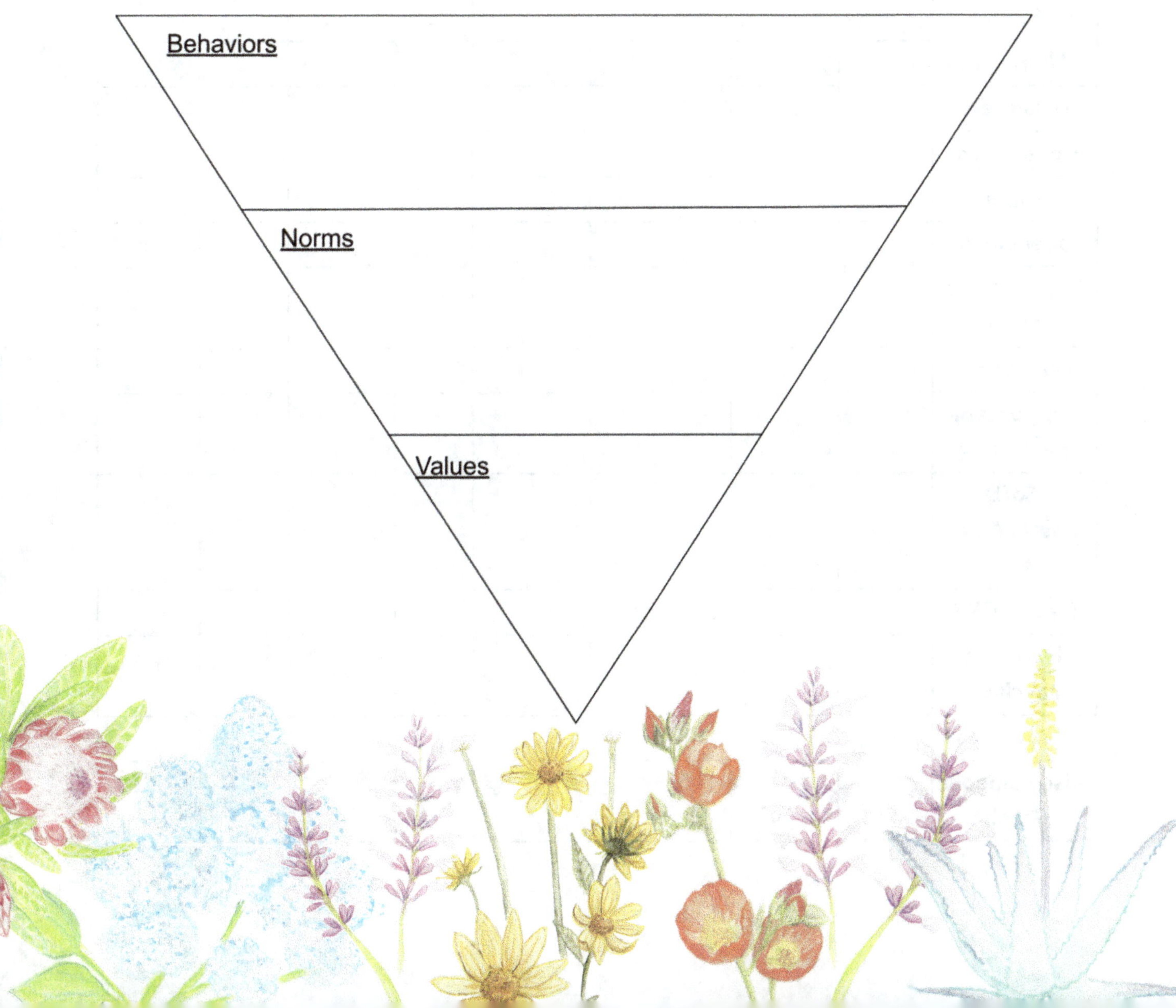

Waste Audit

How much trash do you think you create in one day? ______

x 7

1 week = ______

Which type of trash do you anticipate being the most common? ______________

For the next week, log EVERY piece of trash you throw away using tally marks in the table below.

Item	Monday	Tuesday	Wednesday	Thursday	Friday	Saturday	Sunday	Weekly Totals
Steel								
Aluminum								
Glass Jars								
Broken Glass								
Paper								
Paper carton								
Organics and Food								
Yard waste								
Compostable packaging								
Soft plastic #2 or #4								
Plastic CRV								
Plastic- not recyclable								
Hazardous								
Miscellaneous Trash								

1. What was the most common item and why do you think that is?

____
____
____
____
____
____

2. What did you notice while doing the waste audit? Did your behaviors change at all while you were filling it out?

____
____
____
____
____
____

3. List a few ideas of how you could reduce some of your waste in the future:

1. ____
____
2. ____
____
3. ____
____

Just for Fun

Draw a picture of your future sustainable life!

Design Your Own Canvas Tote

Crossword Puzzle & Word Search

USE THE CLUES TO FILL IN THE WORDS BELOW

ACROSS

3. Taking care of something
4. Putting something in the recycle bin without knowing if it can be recycled or not
5. Finding a new use for something
7. All the different types of life in an area
8. Another word for trash
9. Using less

DOWN

1. Decayed organic material used as a plant fertilizer
2. The produce of the decomposition process using worms
5. Putting paper, metal or glass in a blue bin where it can get remade into something else
6. A greenhouse gas

```
V E Z U X X E B L Q S S T E W A R D S H I P H Q P Y U C U G D Y S X B
V X J Q A T R I C C T V K O O P Q G A E Y R I X G F C A P I R L O P Q
Q E G I O G S O J C C A X F T N S L E Y G U O K C O S Q G T Z N Y O M
V U V D U H Q D P C K J U F Y C O J T J Y B G A S R W F R P T F Q C O
E G G I T H F I U L F Q F N I J I F H U W H R R X M M M L E C U O D C
U W Q X G P A V Z J K E A R J M U Z L X J B H Y E A V G G Y I R R P V
Y E S J G G E E Q N T M P F J M X V C X O U U F P P U D R A G M J C E
M K S S E I C R Z R U A M U B S D G N N W G B T J P U Y Z A U W E M G
G Z K E D B X S L H V B X M F Z H S E P W Z Y Q X Z C R N Y Y A N Z E
I P U A R O Z I S Q E N I O N S I U O J Q L R G I A G I P Q W S B W O
T R G R R D V T Y L O V K C K A W Q F Z Z G J C N L C F S O J T J A T
L S P L U R G Y C B A T O G K A G Z A T X H A U E A I Z Z W S E W S N
P A O Q B J S Y V B G O S K H Z Z Z H M C R I H N T J C N X R E S D K
G I U P X D C N K N G W D C D Y T O N Y W G V S X F R N G P X T Y V L
D P E H M H R F E U F Q Z V W N U O U I I T A Z J U B F C F O P C C T
G R C V S O T M M M Y D E H W E I F F P T Z E C O N L L V F E O Q M X
L J W I X T C A H A D H W V G B M J L D X Y I H N U E P X O K J E N Q
Q E W B A U W I V J W X B V P Q A S X N J B D X M H F M Y P K S P P T
N D P I Y T G D M X E G P C U X V W V X M D C P T N W E W B E T R A P
M Z E W V I W N C R N Y V B A X Y E R T P T D U E Q Y H X J L P S Q E
X L N V Q K U H I U E E R Y W E L C Y C E R L Y W L T V H N N C Y B P
C X W K T E B G M W Z V T O Z H V I G X D Y P C J B F Q U G G X R I R
J L V L J R S B V I V W Z L A V Y S I A R C S S T M E O N C T E G X N
J L S S F Z B T R K G N N K U V N J Y P Z Q Y Y M J S V S P L A B X
Y S L G B E H A H U H V O G U O T Q H L W Q G A K M C L O X T C P F L
P G M X J K D J H V H C N R H Z U D V L B S L S D Q K P D G I Y M R R
C B O T K J W E T C Z F Z B A E Z Y F N L P B Q P V M R J Z B C R Y C
U A F H K F G R S W P U S X E B D T H V B I B B E O M L P L T P G Z Q
U E W B B K K N P B H M O X W J E J F L M D F C C I J Z Y X D U N W B
G F A T W O F Q W K D R K N O F K Q M M S C M D T H M I U B H T F Y G
U M E S P D R S O T Y X Q S T E D T Q G L E E F N S C K N M W R K Q C
I A M O A B E X Z K W S D H W Q N S Z V O W S G X A I D X L N C F Y B
N Y P Y P P A F H L E W X R U U V E C H I J B I C K L J T E M G T R L
H I T E C H Z V V L P Q Y R E L L I F E R Q D W O O L S V C M S F S Q
S O R N M E W F D D Y I Y U P O B U L S L K C G K B S U V Y U O G E A
```

Biodiversity	Compost	Eco
Carbon	Repurpose	Stewardship
Refillery	Waste	Wishcycle
Vermicompost	Landfill	Upcycle
Bokashi	Recycle	Organic

ANSWERS

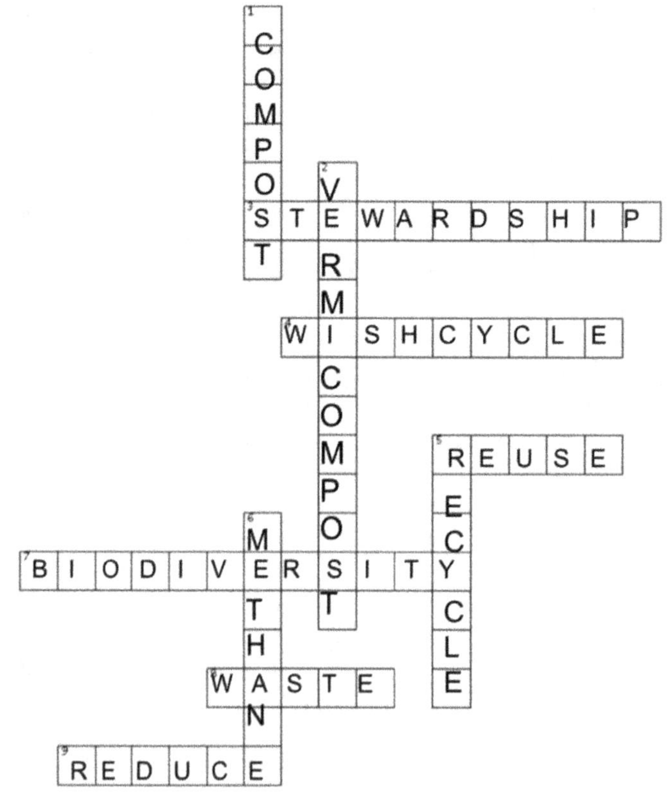

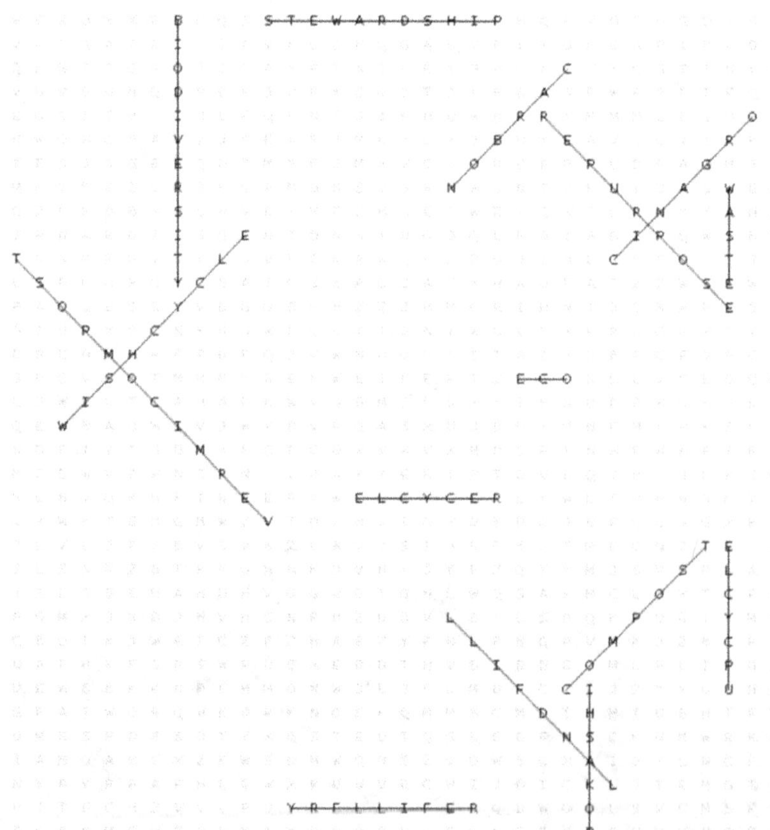

Earth Maze

Find your way to the center of the Earth

Spot The Difference

How many differences can you find in this beach scene?

Today
will be a
gREAT
Day

Trash Sort

Can you put all the trash in the correct bin?

Answers:
Landfill (gray)- Styrofoam, snack wrappers, pet waste, textiles, single-use cups, single-use straws
Recycle (blue)- Junk mail, newspaper, aluminum foil, metal can, glass jar, cardboard box
Organics (green)- Food waste, yard waste, newspaper, cardboard box
Hazardous waste (red)- Wires, paint, battery, broken cell phone

Sticker Fun

Color or design your own fun pictures to cut out.

Upcycle Fun

How would you redesign or paint these old things into something new?

Pages 27-38 of the workbook includes pages that can be cut out of the book to be used as reference. You can put them on your fridge, walls, or scan them and reuse them as needed. Simply cut the page out of the book on the dotted line down the middle of the page:

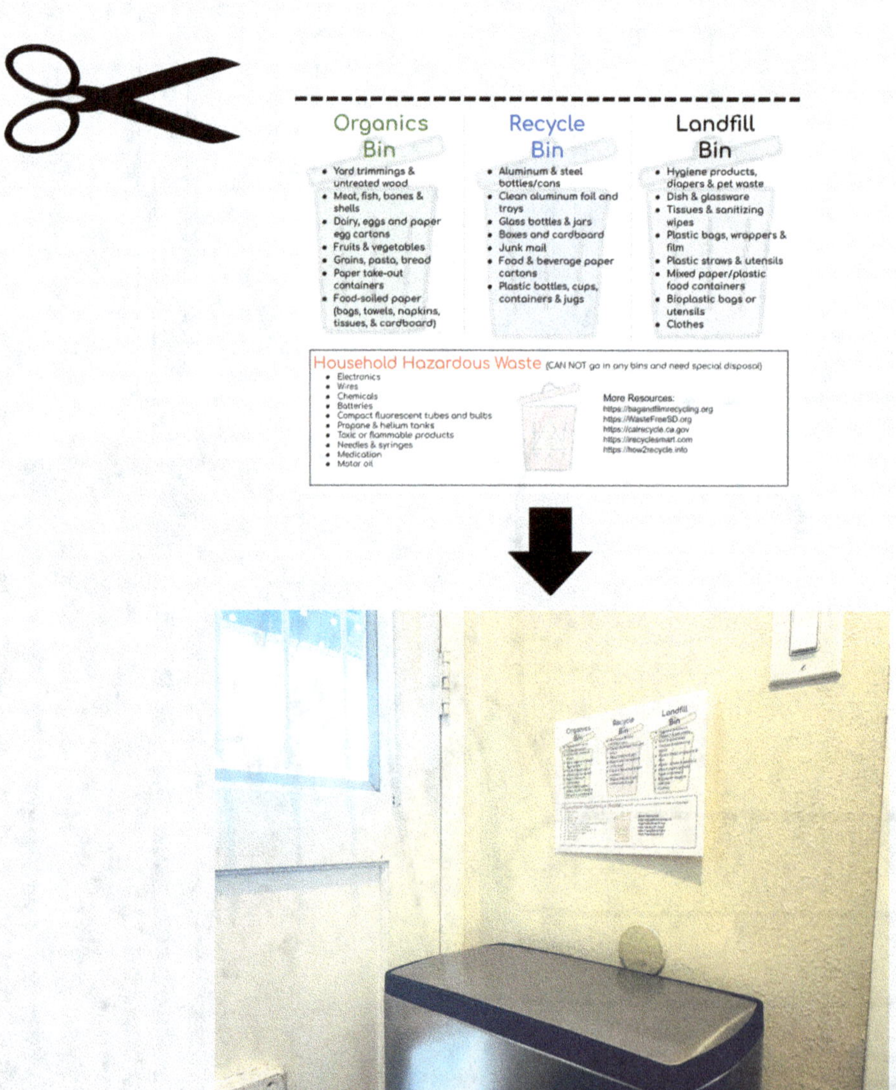

Dirty 12 & Clean 15

Dirty Dozen (recommended to buy organic)	Clean Fifteen
1. Strawberries	1. Avocados
2. Spinach	2. Sweet Corn
3. Kale, collard and mustard greens	3. Pineapple
4. Peaches	4. Onions
5. Pears	5. Papayas
6. Nectarines	6. Frozen Sweet Peas
7. Apples	7. Asparagus
8. Grapes	8. Honeydew melon
9. Hot and Sweet Peppers	9. Kiwis
10. Cherries	10. Cabbage
11. Blueberries	11. Mushrooms
12. Green Beans	12. Mango
	13. Sweet potatoes
	14. Watermelon
	15. Carrots

Organics Bin

- Yard trimmings & untreated wood
- Meat, fish, bones & shells
- Dairy, eggs and paper egg cartons
- Fruits & vegetables
- Grains, pasta, bread
- Paper take-out containers
- Food-soiled paper (bags, towels, napkins, tissues, & cardboard)

Recycle Bin

- Aluminum & steel bottles/cans
- Clean aluminum foil and trays
- Glass bottles & jars
- Boxes and cardboard
- Junk mail
- Food & beverage paper cartons
- Plastic bottles, cups, containers & jugs

Landfill Bin

- Hygiene products, diapers & pet waste
- Dish & glassware
- Tissues & sanitizing wipes
- Plastic bags, wrappers & film
- Plastic straws & utensils
- Mixed paper/plastic food containers
- Bioplastic bags or utensils
- Clothes

Household Hazardous Waste (CAN NOT go in any bins and need special disposal)

- Electronics
- Wires
- Chemicals
- Batteries
- Compact fluorescent tubes and bulbs Propane & helium tanks
- Toxic or flammable products
- Needles & syringes
- Medication
- Motor oil

More Resources:
https://bagandfilmrecycling.org
https://WasteFreeSD.org
https://calrecycle.ca.gov
https://irecyclesmart.com
https://how2recycle.info

Produce Storage Guide

Pantry
Eggplant
Potatoes
Sweet potatoes
Onions !
Garlic
Pumpkins
Winter squash

Counter
Basil
Bananas !
Persimmons !
Pineapple
Pomegranates !
Tomatoes

Counter then Refrigerator
Apricots !
Avocados !
Cantaloupe !
Honeydew !
Kiwis !
Mangoes !
Nectarines !
Peaches !
Pears !
Plums !
Pluots !

Refrigerator

Mushrooms	Celery	Summer squash
Asparagus	Corn	Tomatillos
Cilantro	Cucumbers	Turnips
Dill	Fennel	Zucchini
Mint	Ginger	Apples !
Parsley	Green beans	Blueberries
Watermelon	Herbs	Cherries
Artichokes	Kale	Figs
Beats	Leaks	Grapes
Berries	Lettuce	Grapefruit
Broccoli	Okra	Lemons
Brussels sprouts	Parsnips	Limes
Cabbage	Peas	Mandarins
Carrots	Peppers	Oranges
Cauliflower	Radishes	Green onions
Spinach	Strawberries	

Orange- Fridge shelves
Blue- High humidity crisper drawer
Green- Low humidity crisper drawer

! - Releases ethylene gas as it ripens and causes other produce to ripen too quickly.
These should be stored separately from other products.

*Other notes: Remove greens from produce like carrots as the greens will steal moisture from the root.
**If your greens become wilted, soak in ice water for a few hours in the fridge to add moisture.

Meal Planner

	Breakfast	Lunch	Dinner	Snacks
Monday				
Tuesday				
Wednesday				
Thursday				
Friday				
Saturday				
Sunday				

Shopping List

Produce

- ___________________
- ___________________
- ___________________
- ___________________
- ___________________
- ___________________
- ___________________
- ___________________
- ___________________

Grains & Bakery

- ___________________
- ___________________
- ___________________
- ___________________
- ___________________

Canned

- ___________________
- ___________________
- ___________________
- ___________________

Proteins

- ___________________
- ___________________
- ___________________
- ___________________
- ___________________

Dairy & Plant-based

- ___________________
- ___________________
- ___________________
- ___________________
- ___________________

Spices & Baking

- ___________________
- ___________________
- ___________________
- ___________________
- ___________________

Frozen

- ___________________
- ___________________
- ___________________
- ___________________

Snacks

- ___________________
- ___________________
- ___________________
- ___________________

Condiments

- ___________________
- ___________________

Around the house

- ___________________
- ___________________
- ___________________
- ___________________
- ___________________
- ___________________
- ___________________
- ___________________

Toiletries

- ___________________
- ___________________
- ___________________
- ___________________
- ___________________
- ___________________
- ___________________

Pet Care

- ___________________
- ___________________
- ___________________

Meal Planning & Shopping List

Breakfast options

- ______________________
- ______________________
- ______________________
- ______________________
- ______________________

Lunch options

- ______________________
- ______________________
- ______________________
- ______________________
- ______________________

Dinner options

- ______________________
- ______________________
- ______________________
- ______________________
- ______________________

Snack options

- ______________________
- ______________________
- ______________________
- ______________________
- ______________________

Produce

- ______________________
- ______________________
- ______________________
- ______________________
- ______________________
- ______________________

Grains & Bakery

- ______________________
- ______________________
- ______________________
- ______________________

Canned

- ______________________
- ______________________
- ______________________

Proteins

- ______________________
- ______________________
- ______________________

Dairy & Plant-based

- ______________________
- ______________________
- ______________________

Spices & Baking

- ______________________
- ______________________

Condiments

- ______________________
- ______________________
- ______________________

Frozen

- ______________________
- ______________________
- ______________________
- ______________________

Snacks

- ______________________
- ______________________

Around the house

- ______________________
- ______________________
- ______________________
- ______________________
- ______________________
- ______________________

Toiletries

- ______________________
- ______________________
- ______________________
- ______________________
- ______________________
- ______________________
- ______________________

Pet Care

- ______________________
- ______________________
- ______________________

Recipe Books

Snacks
Personal Care
Cleaning

The rest of the workbook includes dozens of recipes. There are recipes for snacks that can help you reduce packaging and reduce food waste, as well as DIY recipes for personal care products and cleaners.

The intention is for you to be able to cut these pages out and make your own booklets or you can keep them in the book if you would rather.

To assemble the book, simply cut the page out of the book and cut down the dotted line down the middle of the page:

After you have all your pages cut out, you could either staple them or hole punch the corner and add a ring:

Snack Recipes

Roasted Almonds

DIFFICULTY

● ● ○ ○ ○

MAKES _______ 1 CUP

PREP TIME _______ 5 MIN

COOKING TIME _______ 10 MIN

● VEGETARIAN

● LOW CARB

● GLUTEN FREE

● DAIRY FREE

NOTES:

Change up your flavors
by adding honey,
cinnamon or other
spices.

INGREDIENTS

1 cups of Almonds
2 Tbsp neutral oil
Salt to taste

METHOD

1. Preheat oven to 350°F.
2. Like baking sheet with parchment paper.
3. Toss the almonds with the oil and salt and spread flat onto the baking sheet.
4. Bake for 10 minutes, mixing them up half way to help them bake evenly.
5. When the time is up, remove them from the oven and the pan by spread onto a different pan to cool. This stops the cooking process and keeps them from burning.

For sliced or slivered almonds, reduce the cooking time.

REVIEW ☆ ☆ ☆ ☆ ☆

Almond Biscotti

DIFFICULTY ●●●○○

MAKES   15-20 STICKS

PREP TIME   30 MIN

COOKING TIME   60 MIN

○ VEGETARIAN
○ LOW CARB
○ GLUTEN FREE
○ DAIRY FREE

NOTES:

You can add more or less almond extract to taste. You can also use flaxseed meal or egg replacement.

You can make this a lemon almond recipe by adding the zest of 1 lemon and 3 Tbsp of lemon juice. You can also dip them in chocolate or make a glaze to put on top. Combine ½ cup of confectioners' and 1 ½ tsp lemon juice powder (if doing a lemon recipe) and 2 tsp milk; drizzle over cooled biscotti.

REVIEW ★★★★☆

INGREDIENTS

6 Tbsp Butter, softened
2/3 cup Granulated sugar
1/4 tsp Salt
1/2 tsp Almond extract
1 1/2 tsp Baking powder
2 Large eggs
2 cups All purpose flour
Optional add ins

METHOD

1. Preheat oven to 350°F.
2. Using a mixer, beat the butter, sugar, salt, eggs, almond extract, and baking powder until the mixture is smooth and creamy. At low speed of your mixer, add the flour and mix until smooth.
3. Scrape the sticky dough onto the prepared baking sheet with silicone mat or parchment paper and shape it into a log that's about 3/4" thick. I add flour to the top and sides so my hands don't stick to it as I shape it.
4. Bake for 25 minutes. Remove it from the oven, and allow it to cool on the pan anywhere from 5-10 minutes.
5. Reduce the oven heat to 325°F.
6. Use a serrated knife to cut the log into 1/2" slices (be careful to cut them evenly).
7. Return the biscotti to the oven, and bake them for 30 to 35 minutes, until they feel very dry and are beginning to turn golden around the edges.
8. Remove the biscotti from the oven, and transfer them to a rack to cool.
9. Store biscotti at room temperature in an air-tight container for a couple of weeks.

Fruit Leather

DIFFICULTY ●●○○○

MAKES   10-14 STRIPS

PREP TIME   10 MIN

COOKING TIME   5-8 HOURS

● VEGETARIAN
○ LOW CARB
● GLUTEN FREE
● DAIRY FREE

NOTES:

I don't recommend using a fruit with a lot of water like watermelon.

It is possible to just leave the baking sheet out for a few days instead of using your oven but you will have to cover it to keep flies off.

You can also do this recipe in a dehydrator.

REVIEW ★★★★☆

INGREDIENTS

3 cups of Fruit
1 Tbsp Lemon juice
3 Tbsp Honey/syrup

METHOD

1. Blend all ingredients until smooth.
2. Smooth into a rectangle onto parchment paper or silicone baking sheet.
3. Bake on warm or about 200°F for 5-8 hours (baking time will depend on temperature of oven and type of fruit used).
4. When the surface is no longer sticky to the touch, remove and slice into strips using a sharp knife of pizza cutter.
5. Roll up or lay flat in an air-tight container.

Almond Granola

DIFFICULTY

MAKES ___1 LARGE TRAY___

PREP TIME ___10 MIN___

COOKING TIME ___30 MIN___

● VEGETARIAN
○ LOW CARB
● GLUTEN FREE
● DAIRY FREE

NOTES:

A neutral oil that is not flavorful… basically anything but olive oil

Personally, I like blueberries or cranberries for my dried fruit.

INGREDIENTS

- 1/2 cup Neutral oil
- 1/2 cup Honey/syrup
- 1/2 tsp Salt
- 3 cups Rolled oats
- 1 cup Sliced almonds
- 1 cup Dried fruit

METHOD

1. Preheat oven to 300°F.
2. Mix all ingredients together.
3. Spread evenly over parchment paper or silicone baking sheet.
4. Bake for 15 minutes and then stir.
5. Bake for an additional 15 minutes.
6. Cool completely before breaking apart.
7. Store in an airtight container.

REVIEW ★★★★☆

Peanut Butter Granola

DIFFICULTY

MAKES ___1 LARGE TRAY___

PREP TIME ___10 MIN___

COOKING TIME ___30 MIN___

● VEGETARIAN
○ LOW CARB
● GLUTEN FREE
● DAIRY FREE

NOTES:

You can use any type of nut butter for this recipe.

INGREDIENTS

- 4 cups Rolled oats
- 1 tsp Cinnamon
- 1/2 tsp Salt
- 1/4 cup Peanut butter
- 1/2 cup Honey/syrup
- 1 tsp Vanilla

METHOD

1. Preheat oven to 300°F.
2. Pour peanut butter and honey in a small pot on the stove and melt together.
3. Remove from heat and cool. Once cool, add your vanilla.
4. Mix all wet and dry ingredients together.
5. Spread evenly over parchment paper or silicone baking sheet.
6. Bake for 15 minutes and then stir.
7. Bake for an additional 15 minutes.
8. Cool completely before breaking apart.
9. Store in an airtight container.

REVIEW ★★★★☆

Peanut Butter & Chocolate Chip Protein Balls

DIFFICULTY

MAKES — 12-16 BALLS

PREP TIME — 10 MIN

COOLING TIME — 30 MIN

● VEGETARIAN
○ LOW CARB
● GLUTEN FREE
● DAIRY FREE

NOTES:

You can use any type of nut butter for this recipe.

You can use any type of chocolate chip you like. I prefer semi-sweet.

If you don't have mini chocolate chips, just give them a rough chop before adding.

INGREDIENTS

1 1/2 cups Chopped rolled oats
2 Tbsp Flaxseed meal
1/4 cup Almond flour
1/3 cup Mini chocolate chips
1/3 cup Peanut/nut butter
1/4 cup Honey/syrup
1/4 cup Water

METHOD

1. Using a blender, food processor, or slap-chop, blend oats until desired consistency.
2. Add all dry ingredients to a mixing bowl.
3. Mix wet ingredients separately and then add to dry ingredients.
4. Once fully incorporated, form balls by rolling them in your hands (you can also press into a tray and then cut into squares).
5. Put in the fridge for 30 min to chill and store in the fridge in an airtight container.

REVIEW ★★★★☆

Almond & Raisin Protein Balls

DIFFICULTY

MAKES — 12-16 BALLS

PREP TIME — 10 MIN

COOLING TIME — 30 MIN

● VEGETARIAN
○ LOW CARB
● GLUTEN FREE
● DAIRY FREE

NOTES:

INGREDIENTS

1 1/2 cups Chopped rolled oats
2 Tbsp Flaxseed meal
1/4 cup Almond flour
1/3 cup Raisins
1/4 cup Chopped almonds
1/3 cup Almond butter
1/4 cup Honey/syrup
1/4 cup Water

METHOD

1. Using a blender, food processor, or slap-chop, blend oats and almonds until desired consistency.
2. Add all dry ingredients to a mixing bowl.
3. Mix wet ingredients separately and then add to dry ingredients.
4. Once fully incorporated, form balls by rolling them in your hands (you can also press into a tray and then cut into squares).
5. Put in the fridge for 30 min to chill and store in the fridge in an airtight container.

REVIEW ★★★★☆

Cookie Dough Protein Balls

DIFFICULTY

MAKES — 12-16 BALLS

PREP TIME — 10 MIN

COOLING TIME — 30 MIN

- ● VEGETARIAN
- ○ LOW CARB
- ● GLUTEN FREE
- ● DAIRY FREE

NOTES:

You can use any type of chocolate chip you like. I prefer semi-sweet.

If you don't have mini chocolate chips, just give them a rough chop before adding.

If you don't have chocolate almond butter, You can add 1 Tbsp of cocoa powder. You can also use chocolate cashew butter.

INGREDIENTS

1 1/2 cups Almond flour
1/2 cup Chocolate almond butter
1/3 cup Mini chocolate chips
3 Tbsp Maple syrup
3/4 tsp Vanilla extract
1/4 tsp Salt

METHOD

1. Add all dry ingredients to a mixing bowl.
2. Mix wet ingredients separately and then add to dry ingredients.
3. Once fully incorporated, form balls by rolling them in your hands (you can also press into a tray and then cut into squares).
4. Put in the fridge for 30 min to chill and store in the fridge in an airtight container.

REVIEW ★ ★ ★ ★ ☆

Brownie Bite Protein Balls

DIFFICULTY

MAKES — 12-16 BALLS

PREP TIME — 10 MIN

COOLING TIME — 30 MIN

- ● VEGETARIAN
- ○ LOW CARB
- ● GLUTEN FREE
- ● DAIRY FREE

NOTES:

You can use any type of chocolate chip you like. I prefer semi-sweet.

If you don't have mini chocolate chips, just give them a rough chop before adding.

If you don't have chocolate almond butter, You can add 1 Tbsp of cocoa powder. You can also use chocolate cashew butter.

INGREDIENTS

1 1/2 cups Chopped rolled oats
2 Tbsp Flaxseed meal
1/4 cup Almond flour
2 Tbsp Cocoa powder
1/2 cup Mini chocolate chips
1/3 cup Chocolate almond butter
1/4 cup Honey/syrup
1/4 cup Water

METHOD

1. Using a food processor, or slap-chop, blend oats until desired consistency.
2. Add all dry ingredients to a mixing bowl.
3. Mix wet ingredients separately and then add to dry ingredients.
4. Once fully incorporated, form balls by rolling them in your hands (you can also press into a tray and then cut into squares).
5. Put in the fridge for 30 min to chill and store in the fridge in an airtight container.

REVIEW ★ ★ ★ ★ ☆

Date Bars

DIFFICULTY

MAKES 6-10 BARS

PREP TIME 15 MIN

COOLING TIME 2 HOURS

- ● VEGETARIAN
- ○ LOW CARB
- ● GLUTEN FREE
- ● DAIRY FREE

NOTES:

You can use almonds instead of cashews

Flavor options can include cocoa powder (2 tsp), pumpkin spice (1 tsp) or chocolate chips.

INGREDIENTS

1 cup Unsalted cashews
1 cup Pitted dates
1/2 tsp Vanilla extract
Pinch of salt
Flavor option

METHOD

1. Blend all the ingredients in a food processor until it is a sticky dough.
2. Form into any shape and place on parchment paper.
3. Freeze for a couple of hours to retain the shape and store them in the fridge.

REVIEW ★ ★ ★ ★ ★

Apple Sauce

DIFFICULTY

MAKES ONE 16 OZ JAR

PREP TIME 30 MIN

COOKING TIME 20 MIN

- ● VEGETARIAN
- ○ LOW CARB
- ● GLUTEN FREE
- ● DAIRY FREE

NOTES:

You can add cinnamon or other spices at step 4 if you want.

To turn this into apple butter, add the following at step 4: ½ cup of brown sugar, 1 tsp cinnamon, ¼ tsp nutmeg, ½ tsp vanilla, pinch of cloves, pinch of salt

INGREDIENTS

5 Apples
2 tsp Lemon juice
Optional add ins

METHOD

1. Peel and core apples.
2. Place in a pot of filtered water and boil until soft (about 20 minutes).
3. Remove the apples and put them in a blender. I recommend you let it cool for 20 minutes to reduce pressure when blending. Reserve some water from boiling to add to the blender if necessary.
4. Add 2 tsp lemon juice and blend until desired consistency, adding reserved water as needed.

REVIEW ★ ★ ★ ★ ★

Crackers

DIFFICULTY

MAKES — DEPENDS ON SIZE

PREP TIME — 30 MIN

COOKING TIME — 10 MIN

- ● VEGETARIAN
- ○ LOW CARB
- ○ GLUTEN FREE
- ● DAIRY FREE

NOTES:

If you like, chilling the dough can make it easier to roll out.

The tray may need to be rotated depending on your oven.

INGREDIENTS

2 cups of All purpose flour
2 tsp Baking powder
1 tsp Baking soda
1 Tbsp Sugar
6 Tbsp Cold butter
2 tsp Olive oil
2/3 cup Water
3 Tbsp Melted butter
1 tsp Salt

METHOD

1. Preheat oven to 400°F.
2. Add all dry ingredients together in a food processor or mix with a dough blender by hand.
3. Add the cold butter pieces and then the olive oil.
4. Roll the dough as thin as possible on parchment paper or silicone mat.
5. Spread the melted butter on top.
6. Using a pizza cutter, slice the dough into squares, then push a hole into the center of each one using a toothpick or fork.
7. Sprinkle with salt and bake for 10 minutes or until golden brown.

REVIEW ★ ★ ★ ★ ☆

Fruit and Veggie Protein Muffins

DIFFICULTY

MAKES — 15 MUFFINS

PREP TIME — 30 MIN

COOKING TIME — 15 MIN

- ○ VEGETARIAN
- ○ LOW CARB
- ○ GLUTEN FREE
- ● DAIRY FREE

NOTES:

You can also use carrots or combine carrot and zucchini.
You can also use flax meal or egg replacement.
You can also use other high protein flours like almond, chickpea or coconut in any combination.
Add in nuts, dried fruit or chocolate chips.
You can also make this a loaf. Cook at the same temp for 50-60 minutes.

INGREDIENTS

2 cups of Grated zucchini
(about 1 zucchini, not squeezed)
2 Large ripe bananas- mashed
1 Egg
1/2 cup Maple syrup
1 tsp Cinnamon
2 tsp Baking powder
1 tsp Baking soda
1 tsp Salt
2 1/4 cup whole wheat flour
1/2 cup of optional add in

METHOD

1. Preheat oven to 350°F.
2. Mix all your wet ingredients except zucchini.
3. Mix all your dry ingredients and then add to the wet and lastly the grated zucchini.
4. Bake for 15 in muffin tins.
5. Remove from tins and cool on a wire rack.
6. Store in an airtight container at room temp for 4 days or longer in the fridge.

REVIEW ★ ★ ★ ★ ☆

Homemade Uncrustables®

DIFFICULTY

● ○ ○ ○ ○

MAKES — UP TO YOU :)

PREP TIME — 15 MIN

COOKING TIME — NA

● VEGETARIAN
○ LOW CARB
○ GLUTEN FREE
● DAIRY FREE

NOTES:

This is a fun one to have the kids help with!

You can also use a cup if you don't have a crust cutter

INGREDIENTS

Bread
Crust cutter/sealer
Peanut Butter
Jelly
Reusable freezer bag

METHOD

1. Make your peanut butter and jelly sandwich as you usually would.
2. Cut and seal the edges.
3. You can place the sandwiches in individual compostable bags or put them loose in a large freezer bag.
4. When ready to eat, remove the sandwich from the freezer and allow to come to room temperature before eating.

REVIEW ★ ★ ★ ★ ☆

Kale Chips

DIFFICULTY

● ● ○ ○ ○

MAKES — 1 BOWL

PREP TIME — 5 MIN

COOKING TIME — 50 MIN

● VEGETARIAN
● LOW CARB
● GLUTEN FREE
● DAIRY FREE

NOTES:

This is a great recipe if you have kale that is about to go bad.

Change up your ingredients for a salty or sweet variety.

You can rotate your kale while it is in the oven half way through to improve the texture if necessary.

INGREDIENTS

4-6 Large kale leaves
2 Tbsp honey
2 Tbsp olive oil
1/4 tsp garlic powder
pinch of cayenne pepper

METHOD

1. Preheat oven to 200°F.
2. Line a baking sheet with parchment paper.
3. Tear the kale into 2 inch pieces while removing any large stems.
4. Combine honey, olive oil and spices into a bowl and toss the kale in the mixture.
5. Lay the kale on the baking sheet making sure they are not touching.
6. Bake for 50 min until pieces are crisp and flaky.
7. Remove and allow to cool before enjoying.

REVIEW ★ ★ ★ ★ ☆

Personal Care Products

Clay Face Mask

DIFFICULTY

● ○ ○ ○ ○

MAKES   ONE 4 OZ JAR

PREP TIME   5 MIN

SETTING TIME   NA

VARIATIONS

Liquids can include any combination of water, or skin nourishing oil like jojoba, avocado or coconut.

For an added sent, you can add 1 drop of an essential oil when mixing in liquid.

REVIEW   ☆ ☆ ☆ ☆ ☆

INGREDIENTS
2 Tbsp Bentonite Clay
2 Tbsp of activated charcoal

liquid of choice
essential oil (optional)

METHOD

1. Add only the bentonite clay and activated charcoal to your mason jar and mix well.
2.
3. When ready to use, take 2 tsp out of the jar and place them in a shallow dish. Add 2 tsp of your liquid of choice and essential oil.
4. Mix well and then apply to a clean face with a clean finger or with applicator brush. Leave for 15 min or until dry and wash off.

NOTES:
____
____
____
____
____
____

Deodorant

DIFFICULTY
● ○ ○ ○ ○

MAKES ONE 8 OZ JAR

PREP TIME 10 MIN

SETTING TIME 10 MIN

VARIATIONS

If you find that you are sensitive to baking soda you can replace it with zinc powder or possibly use a different essential oil. I find that sage oil is best for my skin.

REVIEW ★ ★ ★ ★ ☆

INGREDIENTS
1/4 cup Arrowroot Powder
1/4 cup Baking Soda
2.5 Tbsp Coconut Oil
Mason jar or empty deodorant container
5 Drops of Essential Oil (optional)
Popsicle stick (optional)

METHOD

1. Mix all the ingredients into a paste and put them into a glass jar or refill an empty deodorant container.
2. Depending on the temperature of your home, you may need more or less coconut oil.
3. If you use a glass jar, consider also using a popsicle stick to avoid having to put your fingers in the jar.
4.

NOTES:

____
____
____
____
____

Bug Spray

DIFFICULTY
● ○ ○ ○ ○

MAKES 1 SPRAY BOTTLE

PREP TIME 10 MIN

SETTING TIME NA

VARIATIONS

You can substitute rosemary for thyme, or you can use both.

REVIEW ★ ★ ★ ★ ☆

INGREDIENTS
2 Tbsp Witch Hazel
2 Tbsp Fractionated Coconut Oil
15 each of Cedarwood, Lavender, Rosemary/Thyme, & Tea Tree
30 Citronella
2 oz. Dark colored spray bottle

METHOD

Mix all ingredients into a dark colored spray bottle (this helps to preserve the essential oils).

Shake well before using.

NOTES:

____
____
____
____
____

Detangler Spray

DIFFICULTY ●●○○○

MAKES 1 SPRAY BOTTLE

PREP TIME 10 MIN

SETTING TIME NA

INGREDIENTS
- 2 Cups Warm Water
- 1/2 Cup Conditioner
- 5 Drops each of Tea Tree Oil and Geranium Oil
- 16 oz Spray Bottle

METHOD

Fill a spray bottle with one of the two essential oil combinations depending on your personal preference.

VARIATIONS

Instead of Tea tree and geranium oil, you can use 5 Drops Each of Ylang Ylang, Lavender and Rosemary.

Jojoba and apple cider vinegar are also good additives.

REVIEW ★★★★☆

NOTES:

____

____

____

____

____

Sunscreen

DIFFICULTY ●●●○○

MAKES ONE 8 OZ JAR

PREP TIME 20 MIN

SETTING TIME 10 MIN

INGREDIENTS
- 1/4 cup coconut oil
- 2 Tbsp powdered zinc oxide
- 1/4 cup pure aloe vera gel
- 25 drops walnut extract oil
- 1 cup shea butter or lotion
- Mason jar or container

METHOD

1. Combine all ingredients, except the zinc oxide and aloe vera gel, in a medium saucepan. Let the shea butter and oils melt together at medium heat. Let cool for several minutes before stirring in aloe vera gel (must be 50 percent or higher pure aloe).
2. Cool completely before adding zinc oxide. Mix well to make sure the zinc oxide is distributed throughout.
3. Store in a glass jar, and keep in a cool, dry place until you're ready to use.

VARIATIONS

You can replace walnut oil with almond oil.

You may want to add some beeswax or another waxy substance for a stickier consistency.

REVIEW ★★★★☆

NOTES:

____

____

____

____

____

Anti-itch Roller

DIFFICULTY
● ○ ○ ○ ○

MAKES   1 ROLLER

PREP TIME   5 MIN

SETTING TIME   NA

VARIATIONS

INGREDIENTS
4 drops Lavender Essential Oil
3 drops Chamomile Essential Oil
3 drops Tea Tree Oil
Fractionated Coconut Oil
10 ml Roll-On bottle

METHOD

1. Add essential oils into a roll-on bottle. Fill the remainder of the bottle with fractionated coconut oil. Place roller insert and cap on and swirl oils together to blend.
2. To use, first cleanse the bug bite area with soap and water, pat dry. Roll directly on and around the bug bite. Let it air dry.
3. Don't Scratch!

REVIEW ★ ★ ★ ★ ☆

NOTES:

Facial Toner

DIFFICULTY
● ○ ○ ○ ○

MAKES   1 SPRAY BOTTLE

PREP TIME   5 MIN

SETTING TIME   NA

VARIATIONS

INGREDIENTS
About 2 oz. Witch Hazel
3 Drops of Lavender Oil
2 Drops of Tea Tree Oil
3 Drops of Frankincense Oil
2 oz Dark Colored Spray Bottle

METHOD

1. First, place all the essential oils into the spray bottle (the dark color helps to preserve the essential oils), then fill the bottle with witch hazel.
2. Clean your face prior to using. Use once or twice per day.

REVIEW ★ ★ ★ ★ ☆

NOTES:

Makeup Remover

DIFFICULTY
● ● ○ ○ ○

MAKES   ONE 8 OZ JAR

PREP TIME   20 MIN

SETTING TIME   5 MIN

VARIATIONS

When choosing your essential oil, lavender, lemon or frankincense are great for you skin

REVIEW ★ ★ ★ ★ ☆

INGREDIENTS
Mason jar
Small cloth wipes or reusable rounds
2 Tbsp of fractionated coconut oil
1 tsp of castile soap
1/2 cup of witch hazel
2-4 drops of essential oil

METHOD

1. Place your cloth wipes or reusable rounds in your jar. In a separate bowl, mix the coconut oil, essential oil and castile soap.
2. Pour over your wipes until all the moisture is absorbed. Lastly, pour just enough witch hazel over the wipes to wet them.
3. Put the lid on the jar and shake to evenly distribute the witch hazel.

NOTES:

Oatmeal Face Mask

DIFFICULTY
● ○ ○ ○ ○

MAKES   ONE MASK

PREP TIME   5 MIN

SETTING TIME   15 MIN

VARIATIONS

REVIEW ★ ★ ★ ★ ☆

INGREDIENTS
1 Tbsp ground oatmeal
1/2 ripe banana
1 Tbsp plain yogurt

METHOD

Mash your banana and then mix in the ground oatmeal and yogurt. Apply to your face and leave for 15 minutes before washing off.

NOTES:

Lotion Bar

DIFFICULTY 

MAKES _____ 3-5 BARS _____

PREP TIME _____ 20 MIN _____

SETTING TIME _____ 20 MIN _____

VARIATIONS

> When choosing your essential oil, lavender, lemon or frankincense are great for you skin
>
> If you don't have one you can use a glass bowl, or mason jar in water.

REVIEW ★ ★ ★ ★ ☆

INGREDIENTS

6 Tbsp cocoa butter
1 Tbsp of shea butter
1 Tbsp of almond oil
5 drops of essential oil
Silicone molds
1 tsp of vitamin E oil (optional)

METHOD

1. Combine all the ingredients except the essential oil into a double boiler. Once the ingredients are melted remove them from the heat and cool slightly.
2. Add desired essential oils and vitamin E and mix. Pour into silicone molds. (Depending on the size of your mold, you can make more or less)
3. Cool completely before removing.

NOTES:
____
____
____
____
____

Toothpaste

DIFFICULTY 

MAKES _____ ONE 8 OZ JAR _____

PREP TIME _____ 10 MIN _____

SETTING TIME _____ NA _____

VARIATIONS

> Add more water if you want your paste thinner. recommended essential oils: Cinnamon(ANTI FUNGAL, antibacterial), Spearmint (antiseptic), and Thieves oil (ANTI INFLAMMATORY, antibacterial)

REVIEW ★ ★ ★ ★ ☆

INGREDIENTS

1/2 cup bentonite clay powder (food grade)
1/8 tsp unrefined high-mineral salt
2 tsp baking soda
2/3 cup water
1/4 cup coconut oil
1-4 drops of essential oils
1 tsp Stevia (optional)
Mason Jar

METHOD

Combine all the ingredients and transfer to a mason jar.

NOTES:
____
____
____
____
____

Mouthwash

DIFFICULTY ●○○○○

MAKES ONE 8 OZ JAR

PREP TIME 10 MIN

SETTING TIME NA

VARIATIONS

Recommended essential oils:
Spearmint, Peppermint or tea tree

Optional Sweetener:
xylitol

REVIEW ★★★★☆

INGREDIENTS

1 cup alcohol-free witch hazel
4 drops Thieves oil
2 tsp baking soda
Dark or amber container
Additional Essential oils (optional)
Sweetener (optional)

METHOD

Mix all the ingredients together in the amber container.
Shake well before using.

NOTES:

____
____
____
____
____

Honey Sugar Scrub

DIFFICULTY ●○○○○

MAKES ONE 8 OZ JAR

PREP TIME 10 MIN

SETTING TIME NA

VARIATIONS

You can use white or brown sugar

You can choose another skin nourishing essential oil like rosemary, Frankincense or lemon
Get creative!

REVIEW ★★★★☆

INGREDIENTS

1 cup organic cane Sugar
1/2 cup extra virgin olive oil
3 Tbsp honey
1 Tbsp aloe vera gel
10 drops lavender
Mason Jar

METHOD

1. Mix all the ingredients in a bowl and transfer to a mason jar.
2. Store in a dark place like the medicine cabinet or under the sink.
3. Great to use on hands, feet, face or before shaving.

NOTES:

____
____
____
____
____

Activated Charcoal Scrub

DIFFICULTY
● ○ ○ ○ ○

MAKES   ONE 4 OZ JAR

PREP TIME   10 MIN

SETTING TIME   NA

VARIATIONS

> 2 activated charcoal capsules is equal to 1/2 tsp of powder

REVIEW ★ ★ ★ ★ ☆

INGREDIENTS
1/3 cup organic cane sugar
2 Tbsp extra virgin olive oil
2 activated charcoal capsules
Mason Jar
3 drops essential oil (optional)

METHOD

1. Mix all the ingredients in a bowl and transfer to a mason jar.
2. Store in a dark place like the medicine cabinet or under the sink.
3. Great to use on hands, feet, face or before shaving.

NOTES:

____

Almond Exfoliator Scrub

DIFFICULTY
● ● ○ ○ ○

MAKES   ONE 8 OZ JAR

PREP TIME   20 MIN

SETTING TIME   NA

VARIATIONS

> Good liquids to add when you are ready to use it include water, sweet almond oil, jojoba oil, or olive oil.

REVIEW ★ ★ ★ ★ ☆

INGREDIENTS
1/4 cup old-fashioned rolled oats
1/4 cup raw, unsalted almonds
1 tsp mineral-rich, fine salt
Blender
Mason Jar

METHOD

Blend the almonds and oats in a blender until the ingredients resemble a flour-like texture. Add the salt and pulse to combine.
Add to your mason jar.

To use, combine 1 tablespoon of powder with 1-2 teaspoons of liquid of choice. Once mixed, gently massage the exfoliator on the face and/or body. Rinse with a warm, damp washcloth.

NOTES:

____

Honey Face Wash

DIFFICULTY ● ○ ○ ○ ○

MAKES ONE 8 OZ PUMP BOTTLE

PREP TIME 5 MIN

SETTING TIME NA

VARIATIONS

> Good oils to use include , sweet almond oil, jojoba oil, Avocado oil or olive oil.

REVIEW ★ ★ ★ ★ ☆

INGREDIENTS
1/3 cup castile soap
1/3 cup honey
3 Tbsp water
2 Tbsp oil
Soap dispenser

METHOD

1. Add the water first to the soap dispenser then the liquid castile soap, honey, and oil.
2. Mix the ingredients together slowly to avoid making bubbles until the honey is fully dissolved.

NOTES:

____
____
____
____
____

Lip Balm

DIFFICULTY ● ● ● ● ○

MAKES 3 TUBES

PREP TIME 20 MIN

SETTING TIME 10 MIN

VARIATIONS

> You can use a double boiler if you are making a larger quantity of this recipe.
> Other butters include mango butter or cocoa butter.
> Oils can be olive oil, jojoba oil, almond oil or coconut oil.

REVIEW ★ ★ ★ ★ ☆

INGREDIENTS
1 Tbsp unrefined shea butter
1 Tbsp oil
1-2 tsp beeswax pellets (about 5g)
1/4 tsp of lanolin or vitamin E (optional)
5 drops of peppermint essential oil (optional
Lip balm tubes or small containers

METHOD

1. Boil an inch of water in a small pot.
2. Fill a mason jar with the butter of your choice, oil of your choice, and beeswax.
3. Heat until the beeswax and butter are melted, stirring occasionally.
4. Turn off the heat and remove the jar from the pot.
5. Working quickly, pour the mixture into a lip balm containers, and allow the balm to sit until formed.
6. Store in cool areas.

NOTES:

____
____
____
____
____

Lip Scrub

DIFFICULTY ● ○ ○ ○ ○

MAKES SMALL CONTAINER

PREP TIME 5 MIN

SETTING TIME NA

VARIATIONS

Replace honey with maple syrup

REVIEW ★ ★ ★ ★ ☆

INGREDIENTS

3 tsp organic cane sugar
1 pinch ground cinnamon
1 pinch ground nutmeg
1/2 tsp pure honey
1/2 tsp coconut oil
2 drops pure vanilla extract
Mason Jar

METHOD

1. Stir the sugar, cinnamon, and nutmeg together in a small bowl.
2. Add the honey, coconut oil, and vanilla extract, and mash it all together.
3. Keep working it until you end up with a thick, fragrant, sugary paste.

NOTES:

Dry Shampoo

DIFFICULTY ● ○ ○ ○ ○

MAKES ONE 4 OZ JAR

PREP TIME 5 MIN

SETTING TIME NA

VARIATIONS

You can also use corn starch instead of arrowroot powder. Color choices include cinnamon, cocoa powder, bentonite clay or activated charcoal. Essential oil choices include tea tree, lavender, rosemary and Geranium.

REVIEW ★ ★ ★ ★ ☆

INGREDIENTS

3 Tbsp arrowroot powder
1-2 Tbsp of color choice (as needed)
6 drops of essential oil of choice
Mason jar
Applicator brush (optional)

METHOD

1. Add all the ingredients to your mason jar and mix well.
2. Use a large make up brush, shaving brush or your hair brush to incorporate it into oily sections.
3. Use only 1 or 2 times per week to maintain healthy hair and scalp.

NOTES:

Cleaning Recipes

Soft Cleaning Scrub

DIFFICULTY

● ● ● ● ●

MAKES ONE 8 OZ JAR

PREP TIME 5 MIN

SETTING TIME NA

VARIATIONS

> Thieves oil is a blend of many essential oils. you can either purchase it or make it yourself.

REVIEW ★ ★ ★ ★ ★

INGREDIENTS

1 cup Baking soda
2 Tbsp Castile soap
15 drops Thieves oil
Water
Mason jar

METHOD

Combine baking soda, Castile soap and Thieves oil into a bowl or mason jar. Add enough water to make a smooth paste.

NOTES:

____
____
____
____
____
____

All Purpose Cleaner

DIFFICULTY
● ○ ○ ○ ○

MAKES — 1 SPRAY BOTTLE

PREP TIME — 10 MIN

SETTING TIME — 1-4 WEEKS

VARIATIONS

> You can use other types of citrus including oranges, clementines, or grapefruit.

REVIEW ★ ★ ★ ★ ☆

INGREDIENTS
Large jar or container
About 4 lemons worth of rinds
(enough to fill the jar)
White vinegar
Water

METHOD

1. Add lemon rinds to a jar, cover with white vinegar, seal and store in a cupboard for 1-4 weeks.
2. Strain into a spray bottle and top off with water.
3. Spray on surfaces and leave for a few minutes for a deeper clean.
4. Avoid use on marble, stone or granite surfaces.
5. This is a disinfectant and works against bacteria but is not proven effective on viruses.

NOTES:
____
____
____
____
____

Toilet Cleaner

DIFFICULTY
● ○ ○ ○ ○

MAKES — 1 APPLICATION

PREP TIME — 2 MIN

SETTING TIME — NA

VARIATIONS

REVIEW ★ ★ ★ ★ ☆

INGREDIENTS
1 cup vinegar
1/8 cup baking soda

METHOD

1. Pour in some vinegar and a good shake of baking soda.
2. Leave to sit for a few minutes then scrub with the toilet brush.

NOTES:
____
____
____
____
____

Laundry Detergent

DIFFICULTY
● ● ○ ○ ○

MAKES ONE 32 OZ JAR

PREP TIME 15 MIN

SETTING TIME NA

VARIATIONS

Soap flakes can be zote, ivory or castile

REVIEW ★ ★ ★ ★ ☆

INGREDIENTS
2 cups Borax
2 cups washing Soda
1 cup grated pure soap flakes
mason jar

METHOD

1. Start by grating the soap using a cheese grater.
2. Mix borax, washing soda and grated pure soap flakes.
3. Store in a sealed container away from children.
4. For a standard washer, use three level tablespoons per wash load.
5. Use less for small loads and one-fourth cup for extra large loads.
6. For high-efficiency washers (both front load and top load), use one tablespoon per load. Increase to two tablespoons for large loads.

NOTES:

Window Cleaner

DIFFICULTY
● ○ ○ ○ ○

MAKES 1 SPRAY BOTTLE

PREP TIME 5 MIN

SETTING TIME NA

VARIATIONS

Essential oils are just for scent purposes, but you can add peppermint, lemon or orange if you like.

REVIEW ★ ★ ★ ★ ☆

INGREDIENTS
White Vinegar
Water
Spray bottle
Essential oil (optional)

METHOD

1. Depending on the size of your spray bottle, Mix together 1 part white vinegar to 4 parts water.
2. using a microfiber cloth, spray on your windows or mirrors to polish and clean.

NOTES:

Air Freshener

DIFFICULTY
●○○○○

MAKES   1 SPRAY BOTTLE

PREP TIME   5 MIN

SETTING TIME   NA

VARIATIONS

Essential oils can be any sent you choose.

You can use any spray bottle but you can also purchase misting spray bottles to diffuse the sent more evenly.

INGREDIENTS
2 oz of filtered Water
10 drops of Essential oils
2 oz Spray bottle

METHOD

Fill a spray bottle up with water and 10 drops of your favorite essential oils. A dark spray bottle will preserve the sent longer.

REVIEW ★ ★ ★ ★ ☆

NOTES:

Mold and Mildew Cleaner

DIFFICULTY
●○○○

MAKES   1 SPRAY BOTTLE

PREP TIME   5 MIN

SETTING TIME   30 MIN

VARIATIONS

You can also make a pase with water and baking soda (50/50 water to baking soda) or use hydrogen peroxide (50/50 water to hydrogen peroxide)

INGREDIENTS
2 cups White vinegar
2 tsp of Tea Tree Oil
Spray bottle

METHOD

1. Fill a spray bottle with white vinegar, add tea tree oil and spray the affected area (safe for porous or non porous).
2. Let it sit for around 30 minutes then scrub and rinse off the area with warm water.

REVIEW ★ ★ ★ ★ ☆

NOTES:

Microwave Cleaner

DIFFICULTY
●○○○○

MAKES   1 APPLICATION

PREP TIME   5 MIN

SETTING TIME   NA

VARIATIONS

INGREDIENTS
1 cup White Vinegar
Juice of 1 Lemon
Microwave safe dish

METHOD

1. Pour vinegar and lemon juice into a microwave safe dish and place it in the microwave and switch it on for 2 minutes.
2. Leave the door closed for a further minute or so to steam, then open and wipe down the inside with a damp cloth.

REVIEW ★★★★☆

NOTES:

Liquid Dish Soap

DIFFICULTY
●○○○○

MAKES   1 BOTTLE

PREP TIME   5 MIN

SETTING TIME   NA

VARIATIONS

You can choose any sent castile soap.

INGREDIENTS
Liquid Castile soap
Water
Squirt bottle or pump bottle

METHOD

1. Mix 4 parts castile soap to 1 part water in a pump bottle or squirt bottle.
2. Add the water slowly to reduce bubbles forming.

REVIEW ★★★★☆

NOTES:

Furniture Polish

DIFFICULTY
● ○ ○ ○ ○

INGREDIENTS
3/4 cup of Olive oil
1/4 cup of White Vinegar
Juice of half a Lemon

MAKES   1 SPRAY BOTTLE

PREP TIME   5 MIN

SETTING TIME   NA

VARIATIONS

METHOD

Mix all of the ingredients into a spray bottle. shake well before using.

REVIEW ★ ★ ★ ★ ☆

NOTES:

Floor Cleaner

DIFFICULTY
● ○ ○ ○ ○

INGREDIENTS
1/4 cup of White Vinegar
Squirt of Castile Soap
Hot Water

MAKES   1 APPLICATION

PREP TIME   5 MIN

SETTING TIME   NA

VARIATIONS

For hardwood floors, you can do 1/4 cups of vinegar and olive oil and a splash of lemon juice.

METHOD

Add vinegar to your bucket of hot water with a squirt of castile soap.

REVIEW ★ ★ ★ ★ ☆

NOTES:

Carpet Deodorizer

DIFFICULTY ●●○○○

INGREDIENTS
Baking soda
10 drops of Essential oil of choice
Mason jar

MAKES ONE 16 OZ JAR

PREP TIME 5 MIN

SETTING TIME 30 MIN

VARIATIONS

I saved a parmesan cheese shaker and used that instead of a mason jar for easy application.

Good oils to use include : lemongrass, eucalyptus, peppermint, orange, or a purity blend.

METHOD

1. Fill a jar with Baking soda and 10 drops of essential oil.
2. Shake together and store for use on carpets or other upholstered items when they need freshening up. leave for up to 30 mins and vacuum.

REVIEW ★★★★☆

NOTES:

Oven Cleaner

DIFFICULTY ●●○○○

INGREDIENTS
1/4 cup of Baking Soda
1 tsp of Salt
Water

MAKES 1 APPLICATION

PREP TIME 10 MIN

SETTING TIME OVERNIGHT

VARIATIONS

METHOD

Combine baking soda, salt and some water. Keep adding water bit by bit until you create a paste.
Cover your oven in the mixture and let it sit overnight. Scrub and wipe clean the next day with a damp cloth.

REVIEW ★★★★☆

NOTES:

Chopping Board Cleaner

DIFFICULTY ● ○ ○ ○ ○

INGREDIENTS
Half a Lemon
Salt

MAKES 1 APPLICATION

PREP TIME 5 MIN

SETTING TIME 2 MIN

VARIATIONS

METHOD
1. Sprinkle salt onto the cutting board and use the lemon half to scrub the board clean.
2. Let sit for a few minutes and rinse off.

REVIEW ★ ★ ★ ★ ☆

NOTES:

Drain Cleaner

DIFFICULTY ● ○ ○ ○

INGREDIENTS
Baking Soda
White Vinegar
Hot water

MAKES 1 APPLICATION

PREP TIME 5 MIN

SETTING TIME 10-15 MIN

VARIATIONS

METHOD
1. Pour a good amount of baking soda followed by some white vinegar to your drain.
2. These two ingredients will react together to break down any dirt, grime and grease clogging up the drain.
3. After 10-15 minutes, pour hot water down the drain or turn on the hot water to flush out.

REVIEW ★ ★ ★ ★ ☆

NOTES:

Stain Remover

DIFFICULTY
● ● ○ ○ ○

INGREDIENTS
1 cup hydrogen peroxide
1/2 cup liquid Castile Soap
Spray bottle

MAKES   1 SPRAY BOTTLE

PREP TIME   5 MIN

SETTING TIME   NA

VARIATIONS

You can use vinegar instead of hydrogen peroxide for dark fabrics you can use any liquid soap if you don't have castile.
You can also try sprinkling baking soda and then applying vinegar on top of the stain.

METHOD

1. Mix all the ingredients together.
2. Stir together slowly to reduce forming bubbles.
3. you may want to test it on a small area before applying it to the stain.
4. leave for 5-10 minutes and wash as usual.
5. Works on clothes or carpets.

REVIEW ★ ★ ★ ★ ☆

NOTES:

Fruit Fly Trap

DIFFICULTY
● ○ ○ ○ ○

INGREDIENTS
1/2 cup Apple cider vinegar
Squirt of dish soap
Mason jar
Plastic wrap (optional)

MAKES   ONE 8 OZ JAR

PREP TIME   5 MIN

SETTING TIME   NA

VARIATIONS

METHOD

1. Fill a Jar with apple cider vinegar and squirt in a little dish soap.
2. Leave the jar out near where you see fruit flies.
3. If the smell bothers you, you can poke some holes in plastic wrap and place it on top of the jar with a rubber band.

REVIEW ★ ★ ★ ★ ☆

NOTES:

Pepper Spray for Plants

DIFFICULTY
● ● ● ○ ○

MAKES   1 SPRAY BOTTLE

PREP TIME   15 MIN

SETTING TIME   NA

VARIATIONS

You can use cayenne powder instead of hot peppers.

REVIEW ★ ★ ★ ★ ☆

INGREDIENTS
2 cups water
1 cup hot peppers
1/4 of an onion
6 cloves of garlic
1 Tbsp liquid castile soap
Strainer
Spray bottle
Gloves

METHOD

1. Blend everything together except castile soap in a blender.
2. Wearing gloves, strain the pulp and put it into a spray bottle. Add castile soap and shake.

*Make sure you wash any vegetable or fruit that comes into contact with the spray before eating.

NOTES:
____
____
____
____
____

Weed Killer

DIFFICULTY
● ○ ○ ○ ○

MAKES   1 SPRAY BOTTLE

PREP TIME   10 MIN

SETTING TIME   NA

VARIATIONS

This recipe is for large areas with a pump spray bottle. You can decrease the ratio if you would rather make a small spray bottle.

REVIEW ★ ★ ★ ★ ☆

INGREDIENTS
1 gallon White vinegar
1 cup of Epsom salt
1 Tbsp Castile soap
Large pump spray bottle

METHOD

Mix epsom salt into vinegar until dissolved. Add castile soap and put it all into a large spray bottle.

NOTES:
____
____
____
____
____

Fabric Softener

DIFFICULTY ●○○○○

MAKES ONE 64 OZ JAR

PREP TIME 5 MIN

SETTING TIME NA

VARIATIONS

Good essential oils include lavender, citrus or rosemary

INGREDIENTS
15 drops of Essential oil
1/2 gallon of White vinegar
Mason jar

METHOD

1. Add your oils to the vinegar, replace the lid and shake together.
2. When adding it to your laundry, shake again and use 1/3 cup per load.
3. If you have a front loading washer, use 1/6 cup.

REVIEW ★★★★☆

NOTES:

Thieves Oil All Purpose Cleaner

DIFFICULTY ●○○○○

MAKES 1 SPRAY BOTTLE

PREP TIME 5 MIN

SETTING TIME NA

VARIATIONS

Good essential oils include lavender, citrus or rosemary.

Thieves oil is a blend of many essential oils. you can either purchase it or make it yourself.

INGREDIENTS
2 cups water
1/2 cup distilled white vinegar
1 tsp Castile soap
3/4 cup hydrogen peroxide
20 drops Thieves oil
spray bottle

METHOD

Add all your ingredients to your bottle and gently mix.

REVIEW ★★★★☆

NOTES:

About The Author

Jessica has a master's degree in teaching biology from Miami University in partnership with San Diego Zoo Wildlife Alliance. From 2010-2020 Jessica taught various subjects to both middle and high school students. She was awarded High School Teacher of the Year for the 2015-2016 school year by her school and the Greater San Diego Science and Engineering Fair's Teacher of the year award in 2017.

Currently, she is married to her high school sweetheart and is a full-time mom to her two sons. She volunteers as a coach for her son's little league team, is a trail guide at the largest urban park in San Diego: Mission Trails Regional Park, and is on the Greater San Diego Science and Engineering Fair's management committee where she coordinates teacher training and screens projects for safety and qualification. Through her Instagram (@Nature.Needs.SD) and website (natureneedssd.org), she hopes to continue to promote sustainable lifestyles and environmental stewardship in San Diego County.

About The Illustrator

Devonie loves the Lord and her family. She is a homeschool mom, Registered Nurse, and lover of art and natural beauty. She has had the joy and the privilege of being friends with Jessica and her wonderful family since high school.

The San Diego River Park Foundation

Proceeds from your purchase have benefited the San Diego River Park Foundation.

They are working to achieve their goal by partnering with government agencies such as the San Diego River Conservancy, business and civic leaders, and a wide range of public organizations. By promoting stewardship of the River, facilitating a better understanding of the River's natural systems, and creating appropriate access to this incredible historic resource, the San Diego River Park Foundation is endeavoring to enhance the quality of life in San Diego.

SanDiegoRiver.org
4891 Pacific Highway, Suite 114, San Diego, CA 92110
(619) 297-7380

www.Ingramcontent.com/pod-product-compliance
Lightning Source LLC
Chambersburg PA
CBHW080523030726
47592CB00012B/3450